Usborne

Mindful Activities

Alice James, Lara Bryan and Darran Stobbart

Illustrated by
Jacqui Langeland and Harry Briggs

With expert advice from
Dr. Angharad Rudkin, Clinical Psychologist

Designed by
Freya Harrison and Tilly Kitching

We've chosen music for
some of the pages – look
out for the QR codes.

A guide to being mindful

Being mindful means being focused on the HERE AND NOW. It's all about being "in the moment," and creating a pocket of calm for yourself. Mindfulness is a helpful tool when your brain is busy, or if you're feeling tense or anxious.

You don't need any special equipment or skills to be mindful. It's just a way of approaching things. If you find your thoughts dashing around, mind experts called PSYCHOLOGISTS recommend these simple steps...

find somewhere comfy to sit.

Close your eyes, or pick one thing to look at and focus on it.

Place your hands in your lap or on your knees.

Take some big, deep breaths.

Think about these questions.

Can you smell anything in the air?

What sounds can you hear?

What can you feel under your hands? Soft fabric? Sticky knees?

Are you warm or cool?

Using this book

This book has a range of activities for you to try. Some need pens and pencils, some are just about sitting and thinking, and some are to get up and do.

You don't have to read the book in order, or finish any of it. Just dip in and out, and see what you enjoy.

When I'm cutting, sticking, building or creating, that's when I feel most calm.

This is a QR code. If you scan it with a smartphone camera, it will take you to calming music that you can listen along to. For more activities, visit usborne.com/Quicklinks and type the keywords Mindful Activities. Please follow the online safety guidelines at Usborne Quicklinks. Children should be supervised online.

Breathe it all out

Keeping your breaths slow and steady on purpose is
a really simple way to feel calm and in the moment.
Try out these three breathing exercises.

Slow and steady

Lie down, with your legs bent
and a hand on your belly.

Close your eyes and
breathe slowly in
through your nose...

...and out through
your mouth,

sloooooowly.

Keep breathing in this way.
Feel your belly slowly rising and
falling as the air goes in and out.

Breathwork is an important
part of yoga, an ancient
mindful practice created
in India.

Bumblebee breathing

Breathe in and out through your nose. Make a humming noise as you let the air out.

hmmmmmmmmmm

Try this for a minute or so. Do you like the way it makes your breath gently vibrate?

You can press your fingers over your ears as you hum, to hear the vibrations even better.

By trying to breathe in a specific way, it helps focus your mind and let go of other worries or distractions in your brain.

Flower breath

Imagine you're sniffing a beautiful flower. Breathe in through your nose three quick times...

sniff

sniff

sniff

...and then breathe out through your mouth as loudly as you can.

haaaaaaaaaaa

Repeat this three times. Imagine any tension or stress in your body is being carried away as you breathe out.

Soothing circles

This page is full of patterns for you to color. Take your time and enjoy bringing each circle to life, one by one.

Geometric shapes like this are known as MANDALAS. They are a traditional part of Buddhist and Hindu culture, and the shapes are designed to help focus attention.

You can doodle your own patterns into the empty circles. Or, if you prefer, just fill them with one color!

Scan this QR code to listen to peaceful music as you color.

Unexpected art

Doodle over the blobs on these pages
to turn them into something new.

Doodle anything you like,
using these blobs as a
starting point.

Draw the first thing that comes to mind, and focus on the feel of your pencil on the page as you doodle.

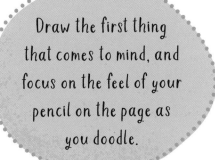

You could blow a splash of watered-down paint across a sheet of paper to create random blobs of your own.

Sit down with a song

Find somewhere comfy to sit, grab a pencil, and put on some music...

For a soothing tune, scan this QR code with a smartphone. Or listen to any music you like.

As you listen, what words or feelings come to mind? What does it make you think? WRITE it down here.

In this big space, DRAW out what's going through your mind. You can use pictures, shapes, shades, squiggles, wiggles... anything. There's no wrong way to draw!

Scientists have found that listening to music can slow down your whole body and be a big mood-booster.

Doodle squares

Use these squares to guide you as you doodle,
draw or write whatever you like.

You could continue with the ideas started here,
or come up with your own designs.

Concentrate on the shapes of the squares, the feel of the page, and the sound your pen or pencil makes as you draw on the page.

Describing sounds

Try making these noises at home. How would you write them down as a sound effect? Try to come up with one word that describes what each noise sounds like.

Rubbing your finger along a leaf

SHOOF

SLOOP

FLAAF

Dropping an apple into a bowl of water

Focus completely on LISTENING to the noise. While you're concentrating on that, you won't be worrying about other things.

Opening a drawer

Popping on a pen lid

Hitting two
pillows or
cushions together

Scraping a
fork across a
cheese grater

A word named after
sound effects is called an
ONOMATOPOEIA (pronounced
on-oh-mat-oh-pee-a).
My favorites are SIZZLE,
JINGLE and SPLOSH.

Flipping through the
pages of a book

Sorting machine

When your head gets full and busy, try sorting through your thoughts by writing them in the different parts of this sorting machine.

How I'm feeling

Stuff I've got going on this week

You can often see things more clearly when you write them down.

I'm worried about...

Questions I'd like answers to

What's further than space?

What do dreams mean?

What would it be like if there were dinosaurs NOW?

Next time your head feels busy, you could fill out these categories on another piece of paper.

Add any other thoughts in here.

Ideas

17

Mindful exploration

Head out for a mindful exploration, and look extra closely to spot things in all the colors of the rainbow. Write down or draw what you find in the spaces here.

Red

Orange

As you explore, PAUSE for a moment to breathe in...
...and outtttttt.
Do that five times.

You could go on an IMAGINARY adventure from inside your home.

Green

Purple

Look UP as well as around. What color is the SKY today?

Yellow

Peace

Harmony

Blue

Peace

19

Lend a hand

Helping someone *else* can make a real difference and give you a warm glow inside. It doesn't even have to be something big. Here are some ideas.

Take the time to ask about someone's day.

Help with chores.

Pick up litter.

Raise money for a charity.

Spend time with someone. You could play a fun game together.

Talk to your family about donating food to a charity that helps feed people in need.

FOOD BANK

What are three helpful things you could do?

1. ....

....

2. ....

....

3. ....

....

Listening with your whole body

If someone you know is upset, you can help them by listening and tuning into how they feel. This means listening with your whole body – not just your ears.

Think about what's being said.

Look at the person talking.

Listen and focus on what they're saying.

Stay quiet and give them time to speak.

Avoid moving too much, so you don't distract them from what they're saying.

Listening can help people feel calm and supported, which is often what they need most in the moment — even more than solutions to the problem.

Try to imagine how they're feeling.

How would you feel if you were in their shoes?

Positivity shield

Imagine this is your shield, and that mean or difficult things will bounce right off it. Use it as a mental tool to help you keep cool and calm.

Work in the first letter of your name.

Doodle on a friendly character, who will help you.

Add some decorations.

Focus on these words and repeat them when you're feeling a little wobbly on the inside.

Take courage

Do your best

Brave as a bear

Draw a dove. Doves have been a symbol of peace for centuries.

You could think of an inspiring message to go on your shield.

Tweet, tweet

Feed the birds

You will need:

* An apple
* Two sticks
* A skewer
* Some seeds
* String

1
Tie two sticks together in a cross shape using string. Keep one end of the string very long.

2
Carefully stick a skewer through the apple. Wiggle it around to make the hole bigger.

3
Stud the outside of the apple with seeds, until it looks like a little seedy porcupine.

4
Thread the apple onto the string, and rest it on the sticks. If it's difficult, make the hole bigger.

5
Then tie the end of the piece of string to a branch. Wait and watch over the next days. Do any birds come to visit?

Hear them sing

Take a quiet break for a while, at home or outside. If you're inside, open up the windows.

Close your eyes and tune in to your surroundings. Can you hear any birds?

How many birds can you hear?

You can normally hear the most birds at dawn and dusk.

Can you pick out different songs – or are they all the same?

If you can't hear any, you can scan this code and listen with a phone instead.

Birds often sing when they feel safe – when there are no storms coming, or predators nearby. That's why birdsong is so relaxing. It has been a sound of peace for people for thousands of years.

Write it out

Take a moment to enjoy playing with some words.

Word bank

Relax

Breathe

Calm

SMILE

Quiet

Star

Mindful

BANANA

WONDER

Spoon

Peaceful

Willow

FOCUS

Space

Word builder

Choose THREE words from the word bank and write them here.

....

....

....

Using any letters from the three words, how many NEW words can you make?

Pick a word...

...from the word bank. Write it here, lots of times, in all sorts of styles. How many different ways can you write it?

Write it tiny, and then REALLY BIG.

Write it using a different pen.

Try chunky letters, and smooth, curly ones.

Write it with the hand you don't normally use.

Write it in another language. If you don't know one, make one up.

Add a picture with one. Color it in.

Did you know?

Being curious and discovering new things is really good for your brain. Which of these facts do you like best? Can you remember it and tell someone else?

It only takes 8.5 minutes for a rocket to get into space.

Ooh la la.

There's a tiny apartment at the top of the Eiffel tower where its designer used to entertain guests.

An octopus can squeeze through a hole the size of a bottle cap.

To reward you for learning something new, your brain releases a chemical messenger called DOPAMINE, which gives you a positive boost.

A limpet's tongue is the strongest living thing in the world – perfect for scraping food off rocks.

Limpet

The biggest waves are beneath the surface of the sea, and can travel for hundreds of miles.

Find out some new facts and
write them down on this page.

Interesting facts often live in...

...books

...newspapers
and magazines

...other
people's heads

...documentary
TV shows

Peaceful patterns

Try continuing this detailed pattern, line by line.
Take your time and don't worry if it's not perfect.

Your brain is wired to find patterns
to help make sense of the world
around you. That's why spotting or
creating patterns is so satisfying.

Scan this QR code with
a smartphone for a
link to a peaceful song
about rain.

Complete these leafy patterns.

Finish these raindrops.

Add lines to these ripples so
they fan out some more.

Move and groooove

Listening to music and letting it sweep you away is a great way to be mindful. Put on some music, and MOVE.

Close your eyes and sway with the FEEL of the music.

Scan this QR code to listen along here. You could put on your favorite songs too or listen to music on the radio.

You might feel a little silly at first, but try to just let go and enjoy it!

Start nodding along to the BEAT. Then let the rest of your body follow along.

Tap your feet. Does the floor feel hard or soft? What sound does the tapping make?

Tap, tap

Lift up your arms and move them. Can you feel them working as you dance and sway? You might feel your heart beating faster too.

Try moving in different ways. FAST. Slooooow. BIG movements. Dainty, elegant ones...

...and freestyle! Which way feels best to you?

Moving your body releases chemicals in your brain called ENDORPHINS that make you feel great. After moving, you might find it easier to be calm and focused.

Paper folding

The art of paper folding, or origami, has been practiced in Japan for hundreds of years. Take a moment to create a butterfly.

1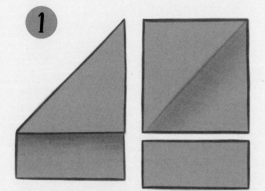

Create a square piece of paper by folding one corner of a sheet of paper up across to meet the far side. Make sure the edges line up exactly. Cut off the remaining paper.

2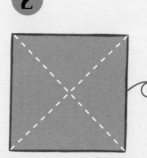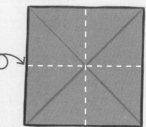

Fold your square into diagonal quarters, and then unfold.

Then turn the paper over and fold it into four more quarters, like this.

3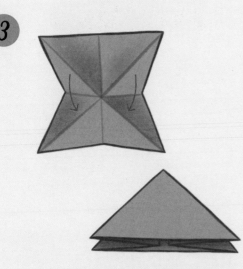

Push the left and right sides of the paper in. The two edges should fold into the middle, turning your square into a triangle.

4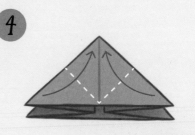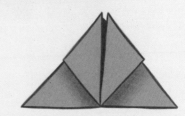

On one side, fold the upper layer into the middle, so the points come together.

5

Flip the triangle over and turn it upside down. Then fold the top layer of the point upwards. Press it flat in the middle – but stop before the edges crease.

Don't worry – the edges should be left curling upwards to give the butterfly its shape.

6

Flip the triangle over again. Fold the point over the top edge. Then, fold the whole thing in half down the middle.

7

Press the edge flat in the spot shown.

8

Release to reveal your butterfly.

Sketching

Collect a few objects from around your home. Then settle down with paints, pens or pencils, and draw them here. Draw them HOWEVER you like – just look closely, and pay attention to all the details.

There's no wrong way to create art, and your drawings don't have to be perfect. Just enjoy the process.

What shape are the objects?

How big are they compared to each other?

Try drawing a different collection of objects here.
You could also try using different pens, pencils or paints.

How many
colors do
you see?

Is light casting
a shadow over
any of them?

What are the objects
made of? Are they
soft, shiny, rough?

Weather watching

The weather outside is always changing, just like your thoughts and feelings. Take a moment to watch the sky, and use the white space on these pages to draw and describe what you see.

Clouds

Can you see any clouds today? What shapes can you see? Do they move and change as you watch them?

Try drawing some of them here.

Go outside and notice how the weather feels on your skin.

Breezy

Cold rain

Warm sun

What else can you feel? Write it down in here.

Wind and rain

Is there any rain today? Is it a windy day? Write about it below.

Drifting by

Watch the clouds as they drift by. Think of your thoughts as being like those clouds. You don't have to do anything about them – just notice them drifting in, and away again...

Is it snowing where you are? Feel the fresh, cold snowflakes land and melt on your face.

Here comes the sun

Color in the sky around the sun with blue or shades of sunset.

Follow the path...

Start

Finish

This is a labyrinth. There's only one path through it. Take your time and enjoy the journey...

Start ↳

Use a pencil so you can erase it and start again.

Finish

While you are busy following these paths, your mind can relax and settle and leave any worries in the background.

Scrap garden

Try growing new life out of old vegetables. This simple method just uses scraps that might otherwise be thrown away.

1

Fill a glass or dish with a small amount of water.

2

Place a veggie scrap on the water. Any of the scraps from these pages would work.

Carrot tops

The bottom of an onion

The end of a celery heart

The end of a lettuce

Point the hairy end down. They'll turn into roots!

3

Come back every day and look for growth. Within a week you should see life sprouting out of the old scraps, and over time they'll grow more.

Growing plants is a slow, mindful activity. You can't rush it — the roots and shoots will grow in their own time.

When the water is running low, add more.

4

When plants have grown green shoots about 5cm
(2 inches) tall, you can plant them in a little pot of
soil, or in the ground, if you have a garden.

Completely bury your
onion bottom in soil.
Over time, greenery will
shoot from the soil and
a full onion will grow.

Celery

lettuce

Onion

Carrot

A whole new carrot won't
grow, but the tops will. You
can cut and cook them for a
healthy food full of vitamins.

Enjoy the process of
coming back each day to
see what has changed.

43

Craft a poem

Poems don't always have to rhyme, or even make sense. Have fun making up a poem here – follow these steps and just see what comes out. Is it silly, funny, or surprisingly meaningful?

1. FIND A BOOK, ANY BOOK!

2. Start your poem with the first two words on the back cover of the book you have found.

3. Start a new line. Now write the first 5 words of the first sentence in your book.

4. Start a new line. Go to page 15 of your book. Write down the first FOUR words from the LAST full sentence on the page.

5. TURN BACK TO PAGE 7 IN YOUR BOOK. ON A NEW LINE WRITE DOWN THE FIRST WORD YOU SEE. THEN THE NEXT TWO WORDS THAT START WITH THE SAME LETTER. PUT A PERIOD BETWEEN EACH ONE.

6. Turn to the last page in your book. Take a short sentence from the page. Switch around a couple of words.

For example...

You can't.
The name for our planet,
Cuttlefish in fighting mode,
Peaks. Parts. Pirates.
We this book bound with twine.

Write out your poems here. Do as many as you like. The more you do, the more likely you are to hit on something that you like. When you finish each one, give it a title.

Hunt for hidden treasures

Take a CLOSE LOOK around your home to find objects in the categories below. Write in or draw the things you discover.

Things that start with:

B

Y

S

Something that makes you...

...smile.

...think.

Objects can have strong connections to emotions. Notice how the objects make you feel and what memories they bring up.

Something unfamiliar might make you CURIOUS. Ask someone about it. What is it? Where did it come from?

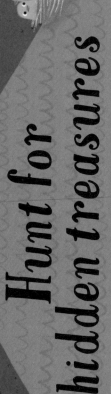

Something that feels...

...soft.

...warm.

...bumpy.

The oldest thing

This will be a real search! Is it older than YOU?

It can be reassuring to look at an old object. It has been around for a long time, and is STILL here for you to enjoy today.

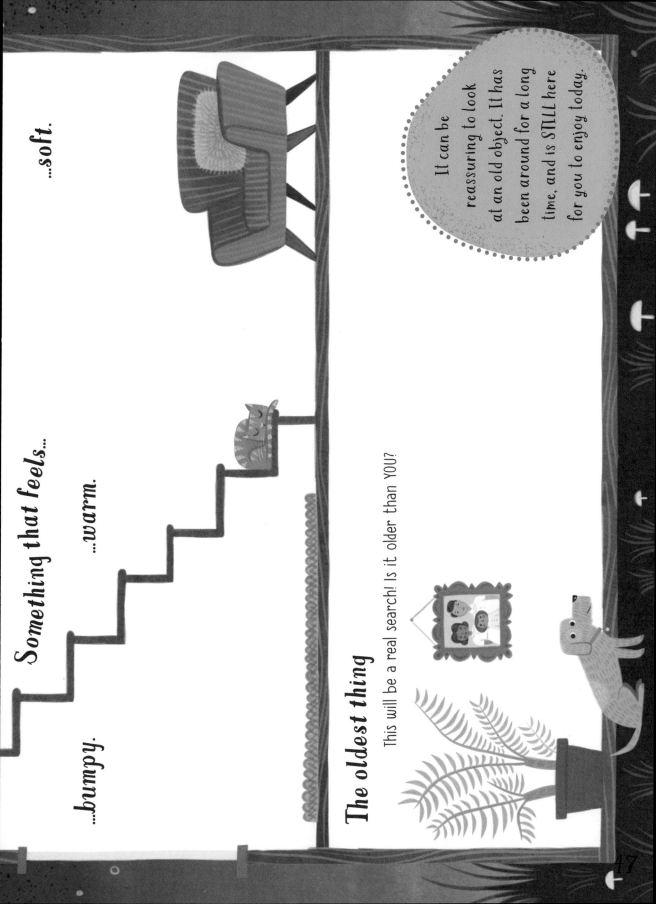

47

Rise and shine!

Write a story

The first sentence is here to get you started. What happens next?

Chapter 1

Far away, as the sun breaks through the trees, someone is just waking up from a very deep, hundred-year sleep.

Create a dawn

Follow the numbers to fill in the scene on the right with these sunrise colors.

Yellow	Orange	Pink
1	2	3

Your body and brain are linked to the cycle of the sun. When the sun rises, it wakes up the cells in your body.

Illustrate part of your story – maybe a character, or the setting.

Ballet moves

Try these simple ballet positions
to get in tune with your whole body.

Finding your position

1 Imagine a string running
through your back and out
of the top of your head.

2 Picture the string pulling
you up, keeping your back
straight and your head up.
Relax your shoulders.

3 Hold your arms
with your
elbows out and
your fingers
level with your
belly button.

Focus on taking
slow, regular breaths
as you hold your
ballet positions.

4 Place the
heels of your
feet together,
toes pointing
outwards.

In ballet this is called FIRST POSITION.

Getting balanced

 Hold your left leg out, and point your toes out straight.

Feel your weight shift onto your right foot as you hold that position.

2 Bring your left leg back, but this time slide your foot so that the heel is nestled in the curve on the inside of your right foot.

This move is called a tendu. Your feet are now in THIRD POSITION.

3 Bring your right arm up above your head, with your fingers open and relaxed.

4 Bring your left arm to join it, framing your head. This is called FIFTH POSITION.

Try holding these positions and thinking about where your body is and how it feels to hold it there.

Scan this QR code for music to practice your ballet poses to.

Balance stones

Building a tower of stones takes focus and a steady hand.
Try it next time you're somewhere with lots of stones or pebbles.

It might take a while to find the right balance. Don't worry if your tower tumbles down.

Feel the weight of each stone as you pick it up. Stack heavier ones at the bottom, and lighter ones at the top.

Remember to put the stones back when you're done.

You could even try this at home... with potatoes!

Lots of things can pull us off balance - being hungry, tired, upset... Pay attention to these clues, so you can work out how to find your balance again.

finish this pebbly pattern by drawing more stones.

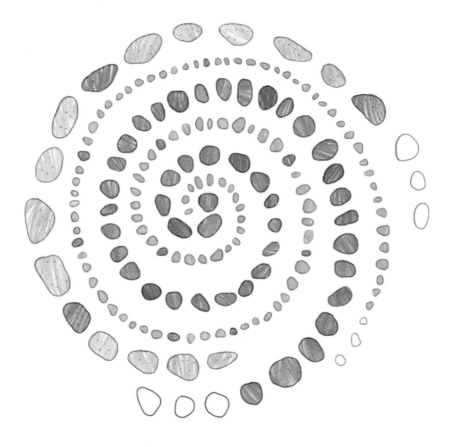

Share a kind thought

Making a card is a simple way of connecting with other people and making them feel good.

fold a piece of thick paper in half and decorate it. Add some words on the front and write a message inside.

You could thank someone who's done something special for you, or for being a good friend.

Wish someone luck if they've got a challenge ahead.

GOOD LUCK

THANK YOU SO MUCH!

Or let someone know you're thinking of them.

Dear Grandma, How are you? I miss you!

How do you want your reader to feel? Take your time and choose each word with care.

Make a heart

Sometimes it's easier to say something with pictures than words.
Try it out with this pop-up heart card.

1

First, fold a piece of thick paper
in half. Then draw a half-heart
shape on the folded edge.

2

Cut along the dotted lines,
without cutting the gap
between the two.

← — Don't cut
here.

3

Open the card and fill the heart
with red. Then push the heart
from behind to get it to pop up.

4

Fold the card in two, with the
heart folding forwards.

5

Now, when you open the
card the heart should pop
up. Decorate the outside
and add a message.

Imagine...

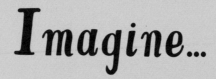

Here are some ideas for little poems
or stories to write, or pictures to draw.
Dive in and let your imagination run wild...

Imagine you are a costume designer
for superheroes. Create some new
looks for them here.

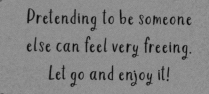

Pretending to be someone
else can feel very freeing.
Let go and enjoy it!

Pretend you are the leader of your
country. Write out a new LAW that you
would bring in if you were in charge.

OFFICIAL
DOCUMENT

Imagine you are a wise, old wizard. You wear a large overcoat, its pockets heavy with things you've collected on your travels. Describe some of the things in your pockets here. You could draw them too.

If you were captain of a ship, what onboard rules would you have?

1.

2.

3.

Write a message in this bottle, and imagine sending it out to sea.

Puzzle away

Take your time with these puzzles and enjoy the feeling of your brain untangling the knots and finding solutions. Turn to page 64 for the answers.

Drawing challenge

Can you draw over each of these pictures without lifting your pencil or going over the same line twice? You can cross over a line.

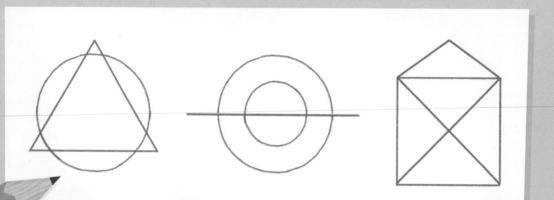

What am I?

See if you can find the answers to these classic riddles.

A

Can you name three consecutive days without using the words Monday, Tuesday, Wednesday, Thursday, friday, Saturday, or Sunday?

B

What comes once in a minute, twice in a moment, but never in a thousand years?

C

The more you take, the more you leave behind.

Search me

Can you find all the words from this poem in this jumble of letters?
Look across, down or diagonally to find them.

By the old still pond,
Suddenly a frog leaps in.
Splash! Silence again.

This is a HAIKU, an ancient
type of Japanese poem.
They're always three lines
long, don't rhyme and are
usually about nature.

Translated from a haiku by
Matsuo Basho, 17th-century poet

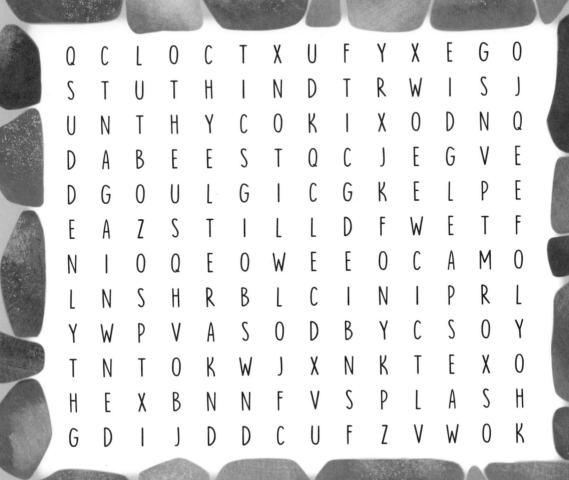

Q C L O C T X U F Y X E G O
S T U T H I N D T R W I S J
U N T H Y C O K I X O D N Q
D A B E E S T Q C J E G V E
D G O U L G I C G K E L P E
E A Z S T I L L D F W E T F
N I O Q E O W E E O C A M O
L N S H R B L C I N I P R L
Y W P V A S O D B Y C S O Y
T N T O K W J X N K T E X O
H E X B N N F V S P L A S H
G D I J D D C U F Z V W O K

Gratitude leaves

Take a moment to notice some of the things or people you feel GRATEFUL for. Jot them down on these leaves.

I'm grateful for...

You don't have to fill the leaves in all at once. Save some for later.

Come back to this page if you need a boost. Remembering the good things can be very reassuring if things feel difficult.

Psychologists have found that focusing on things you're GRATEFUL for can help you feel more positive.

I'm thankful for all the pencils in my scribble box.

Mindful moments

Every day, there are lots of tasks we do without really thinking. But if you tune into your body and what's going on around you, you'll discover your day can be full of mindful moments.

Can you feel your muscles warming up as you start your day?

Imagine each swallow of breakfast sending sparks of energy down through you.

Whooooosh

When you look out of the window, try to notice one new or unusual thing.

What shape is that cloud making?

Who's that bird talking to?

Take a moment to give your food a sniff before you start eating, and see if you can smell all the different ingredients.

TWEET

Fresh sunshiney **LIKE BRAIN BREAKFAST**

When you step outside, what does your first breath of outdoor air feel like?

UNFOGGING

BA BOOM BA BOOM BA BOOM BA BOOM BA BOOM

When you do something active, feel your heart beat faster and your breathing get deeper.

Does time feel as if it's going faster or slower when you're moving quickly?

Having a warm shower can make you feel fresh AND sleepy all at the same time.

ZZZZzzzzzzz

Imagine your toothbrush is saying hello to each tooth it cleans. Each one has done a lot of hard work chatting and chomping today.

Hello!

As you sink into bed, give your pillow a hug. It deserves it for being so comfy and relaxing...

63

Answers

Drawing challenge

There's more than one way to solve these puzzles. But you could draw each one following these steps.

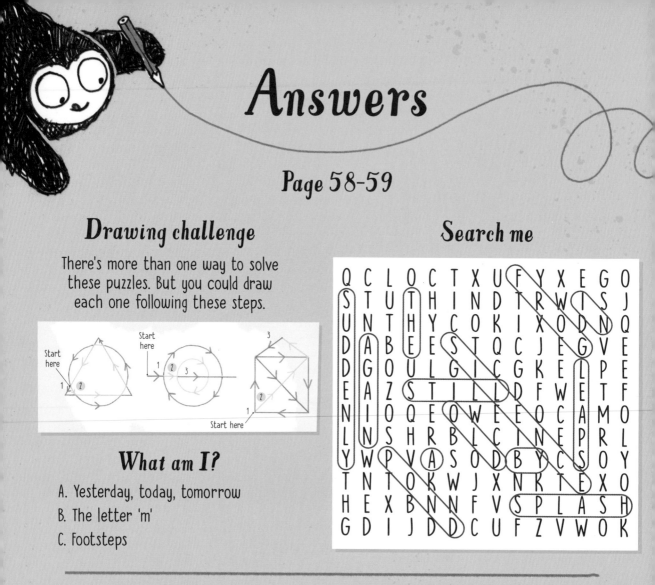

What am I?

A. Yesterday, today, tomorrow
B. The letter 'm'
C. Footsteps

Search me

Design manager:
Stephen Moncrieff

Music consultant:
Anthony Marks

With thanks to
Eddie Reynolds

First published in 2022 by Usborne Publishing Limited, 83-85 Saffron Hill, London EC1N 8RT, United Kingdom. usborne.com Copyright © 2022 Usborne Publishing Limited. The name Usborne and the Balloon logo are registered trade marks of Usborne Publishing Limited. All rights reserved. No part of this publication may be reproduced, stored in a retrieval system or transmitted in any form or by any means without prior permission of the publisher. First published in America 2022. This edition published 2024. AE.

Children should be supervised while online. Usborne is not responsible and does not accept liability for the content or availability of any website other than its own.